With

silent

sacred

holy

deepening

heart

Jerry

For

*Mom & Dad*

and

for

*Yula Claire*

silent

sacred

holy

deepening

heart


em claire

Silent Sacred Holy Deepening Heart

Em Claire

Cover design by Frame25 Productions
Cover art by Maxx-Studio c/o Shutterstock.com
Interior Book Design by Frame25 Productions

Silvergirl Publications
PO Box 1085
Ashland, OR 97520
e-mail: silvergirloffice@gmail.com

Distributed by:
Hampton Roads Publishing Company, Inc.
Charlottesville, VA 22906
www.hrpub.com

Library of Congress Cataloging-in-Publication Data

ISBN 978-1-57174-636-8

10 9 8 7 6 5 4 3 2 1
Printed on acid-free paper in Canada

# INTRODUCTION

There is a tremendous deepening taking place in the heart of Humanity.

If you have been drawn to a book called *Silent Sacred Holy Deepening Heart* for reasons recognized or not yet recognizable, then I know that you have already been asked by Life to open and to surrender to a degree you would not have thought possible; to find courage in the quietest and deepest and most solitary places inside of you . . .

I hope that some of these poems will remind you that you are not so different from the next person: full of hopes and dreams and fears and sensuality and creativity and intelligence and courage and an inherent ability to Love every situation that shows up—which takes some practice. Sometimes the only, only, *only* thing we can do at the end of the day, *is Love*.

When you are seeking reminders of Who You Are in Truth, you may wish to look to the poems in the section of this book called, "Remembering".

If you are feeling the sting of your own tears, wrung from the human experience, you might choose to read from the section called, "Forgetting".

And when you want to fall asleep dreaming of your Beloved, so close that you can smell her scent, or taste the salt of his skin, or be undressed by The Gaze from eyes to soul, then you will want to visit the poetry section called, "Naked".

The word "god" appears often throughout the poetry, as well as Beloved, and Goddess; The One, Divinity, and more, but the name God has also become gentle, easy and familiar to me on a very intimate level, as I have finally and over many years found my own understanding and association with a higher guidance and a profound source of goodness, even though I could as easily say Life, Love, Higher Self, The Friend, The Presence, The Tao and so on. I find that the word "god" also leaves little confusion regarding what I am referring or appealing to when it appears in the poetry.

Let me say this: Give any name to That Source which calls to you, but let it never separate us from one another. There has been far too much of this already and the planet and its people need desperately for all of us to simply Love. Besides, it appears as if we've already tried everything else . . .

I hope that you will find a poem here that might be a lantern in the window to which you have just this moment lead yourself, for reasons your own Self and Soul know.

You are Love; you are Loved,

Em Claire
Ashland, OR
December 2009

*remembering*

God says for me to tell

Nothing needs fixing,

everything desire

a

Celebration

You were made to bev

so that you could

the many miracles at ye

You were made to stro

so that you could disc

own beautiful face of

just above

that you think you au

# SHINE

God says for me to tell you this:

Nothing needs fixing;

everything desires

*a*

*Celebration.*

You were made to bend

so that you could find

all of the many miracles at your feet.

You were made to stretch

so that you could discover

*your own beautiful face of Heaven*

just above

all that you think you must shoulder.

☙

When I appeal to God to speak to me,

I'm feeling just as small and alone as you might feel.

But this is when, for no particular reason at all,

I begin to

*shine*

# WHATEVER IT WAS

It is your own life that you desire to cherish

like one brings the downy tuft of a dandelion to the lips

blows softly

*prays*

to give everything away

*keep*

only what remains

of a life well lived

a life well loved

nourished and blessed

by the suns and by the soils

and by whatever it was

that

finally

*Opened You*

# LIGHTBABIES

We are Lightbabies.

Golden Grace.

*Wings, meant to fly.*

We are delicate and pregnant

with goodness.

We are each made of such a quiet

that the entire Universe

can hear us.

◎

There is only the Unfolding; the Opening

ever happening.

All else are thoughts –

lollipops for the mind.

*We* . . . are *Lightbabies*

parading

as Humankind.

## THE BEST DANCERS

Maybe God keeps me here like this

*to stumble a little.*

If I were to suddenly just

turn into light,

blinding *myself* even

to the most precious and necessary illusions,

*then what hand could hold my own?*

*Where would rest a weary head?*

*What good use for warm hearts;*

*for hot tears?*

*Why eyes to see?*

*Why arms to open?*

*Which Lovefamily to fall into?*

☙

Oh, the best dancers know

what grace

*every* stumble

contains.

# LONG AT SEA

I left my home so long ago now

that I would not recognize my own face.

I constructed the Boat of My Life

and I set out

into the open sea,

waving to all who knew

that the seas would give me

everything I could handle

and everything I could not.

And yet they waved, and I set out

into the open sea

in the Boat of My Life:

built from Soul, crafted by Heart,

and with great innocence I pushed off

into the open sea

and have been away from my home

so long now that I would not recognize my own face

but I know that Home,

*Home*

remembers me.

weet Unveiling is so beca

there is perhaps nothing

more beautiful

The glide that you once

"walking"

Your fears drop

as gently as linge

As Who You Are

naked child

turns every purpose

Lightward

# THE SWEET UNVEILING

The sweet Unveiling is so becoming
there is perhaps nothing
more beautiful

The *glide* that you once called
"walking"

Your fears
dropped as gently as lingerie

As Who You Are
naked child
turns every purpose
Lightward
toward what has always been
right
here
shining
as

*You*

# THE GARDENER

I set out every time the Wanderer.
Yet with each unplanned step
I arrive again
*in the garden of my own heart.*

You've told me countless times
of the plantings here:
closed buds & open blooms
where my own beauty
runs rampant
throughout all of the garden walls.

☺

You see,
a Gardener yearns to be on bended knee
tending *all* that grows;
training *everything*
with Light –

or with both hands
plunged *deep*
into Its fertile ground . . .

# THE LONGING

Do not pretend that The Longing

has not also lived in you,

swinging like a pendulum.

You have been lost,

and thieved like a criminal

your Heart

into the darkness.

But life is tired, Deep Friend,

of going on

*without you.*

It is like the hand of the mother

who has lost the child.

And if you are anything like me, you have been afraid.

And if you are anything like me,

*you have known your own courage.*

There is room in this boat:

*take your seat.*

Take up your paddle, and all of us

*– All of Us –*

shall row our hearts

back

*Home.*

# THINGS WILL BE DIFFERENT NOW

Things will be different now, you know.

Not the snows, blanketing mountains in June.

Not, "The frost came early" or "stayed late".

The kind of different

*that stains the soul;*

that leaves an Innocent dusted

with

*every new color of God.*

⊚

Once you have seen deeply

and been deeply seen

you know that

nothing

has ever, ever been as it seemed;

that your own reflection is

every Christ, every Goddess, every Buddha, and Brahmin

put simply: the *Everyone's Heart.*

I AM THAT I AM

I AM THAT I AM
*and*
*so much more:*
*the Light, the Sound; the Living of God on the Ground.*


*I could show you every feather in the Wing.*
*Every color and hue.*
*Every beautiful thing.*
*But*
I AM THAT I AM
*wants to*
LOVE
*Whatever has not yet known it.*
*Whomever has not yet felt it.*
*However Life's not yet done it.*


*Oh, there is still so much Loving,*
*yet to be found,*
*just*
*Living God on the Ground.*

...we a precious occurre...

as long as we think we

we don't have long

Too much time is being

running

from face to face

...king, "What is my na...

If you don't yet know

or if you're forgotten

then become still, go wit...

and answer it.

## PRECIOUS OCCURRENCE

I am a *precious occurrence*,
and I don't have long.
*We* are *a precious occurrence*,
and as long as we think we have,
we don't have long.


Too much time is being wasted
running
from face to face
asking, "What is my name?"


If you don't yet know it,
or if you've forgotten,
then become still, go within,
and answer it.


You . . . are a *precious occurrence*.
Tell *us* your name.

## LAY THE HAMMER DOWN

God says, *"Lay the Hammer down."*

Which is really my own voice, make no mistake.

And it is *your* own voice, too.

So "lay the Hammer down"

and put your hand to your lips,

or lay it against your heart, whispering

"Sweet forgiveness,"

though there is nothing to forgive.

All we do is try to Love.

It appears as everything: anger, fear, and hurt

of every kind.


*But all we do is try to Love.*


There is nothing to forgive save

*lifting the Hammer* again . . .

# YOU WERE MEANT

*All of This:*

it is preparation for walking in the world

*as Light.*

You have been found now,

and the running of many lifetimes

*is over.*

So as each layer of dust

is wiped clean from the surface,

the You

you have known

*must* disperse.


Let *this* Light become

your Speech & your Silence.


Let the grief

that has lived you

*pass away.*

Let the people

who love You

*Love Themselves.*


Let the Earth shake,

the Stars burn,

the Skies break

when You do:


as painful as this part is,


*You were meant to know your Light.*

# READY

You never really know

when it will come.

Rising, laying foot

into the same imprint

you've made

yesterday

and the day before

and yes,

eternally before.

But some time

that superbly hairline crack

in your well preserved casing

will suffer

*a*

*Grace*.

You can call it crisis, or crumble

*or*

you can see it as
*the first time your truth has succeeded in escaping,*

like the soft and persistent

pressings of a chick

ready to leave the egg

ready to *know* Life

for the first time.

# KNOW YOURSELF AS LIGHT

Know Your Self as Light.

Bigger even, than Breath.

Larger even, than the Whole.

Quieter even, than the Quiet that holds You.


Know Your Self as Held.

Softer even, than as before;

Deeper even, than any Darkness.


When the Lightbody of You

breathes without borders,

knows not

even of the concept,

or of any bounds at all . . .


when you Know Your Self

as only Light

summoning the Mystery

to move through You –

exquisite, innocent instrument

of the long

long, eternity of song


then


Know Your Self as

Life's greatest Laughter;

Life's greatest Lover,

beckoning the Mystery


*come hither* . . .

## BEAUTIFUL DREAMER

Beautiful Dreamer

Who Are You

sitting in the seat of this soul?

Bless your innocent eyes

half closed.

Bless your tender jaw

still set in confusion.

Bless your full, beating heart

so kissed with Light.


Bless the hand that writes,

and the breath that hesitates,

and the World that waits


*for You.*

Here

If you are reading th

your perseverance has bee

and if Grace is winnin

w, hold on loosely to whi

knots on a rope that mar

hand over hand

you will continue to cl

sometimes through ecsta

ometimes through white ag

higher

into evermore ligh

# LOVE ITSELF

Please do not regret

all those moments that have brought you

*Here.*

If you are reading this,

then your perseverance has been answered,

*and A Grace is coming.*

So for now, hold on loosely to where you are.

And like knots on a rope that mark your reaching,

hand over hand

you will continue to climb –

sometimes through ecstasy,

sometimes through white agony, but

*higher*

into evermore light.

This same formula over and over again.

Until that day you find yourself

*just a beacon. Only flame.*

In a place

*where even Love Itself*

has come undone.

## BE RECEIVED

*Move slowly from these old skins.*

Your belly is raw, your back is tender –

you are rudimentary now.

*Move softly from these old skins.*

Let the full bodyweight

of all your innocence

down.

*Be received.*

*Be received by the broad earth of your worthiness.*

Cast off everything

everyone else has known for you.

*Move gratefully from these old skins.*

And this time, if you toughen,

decide

*for whom?*

# SHAMELESSLY

I know that these words may open you

*shamelessly*.

For the surprise element I apologize.

But not for the response.

Never

*for what it is that will be exposed to the light*.

There is that second before a second,

just before you cover and run –

when you hear the lightening of Truth

crackling through your skies

because *Life wants you back*.

I know that these words may open you,


*shamelessly*.

# THE ONE BEING DANCED

Let these words be a whirling dervish, then!

I am unraveled beyond what naked means.

There is simply no place for "me"

when The One

wants so clearly to dance!

So I acquiesce,

and the words present themselves behind my heart

like an ocean of songs

that will not be tamed no matter who

The One Being Danced


*thought she was.*

## THIS IS YOU

In the eye of the Eternal storm of Love

there waits a

Calm.

*This is You.*

A spacious heart

that is

*free to break.*

...ere the Heart is used t...
...he only place where love is
                    a Mind full of joy
draws  the Heart like a
a surprisingly  different
A flame where nothing
        no wings me forfeit
God stretches the length of t...
abide in every room at a...

                    simply

                    because

                    We

# A MIND FULL OF JOY

Whereas the Heart is used to being

the only place where Love is found,

a Mind full of joy

draws the Heart like a moth

into a surprisingly *different* flame.

A flame where nothing burns –

no wings are forfeited.

As if God stretches the length of The Home

to abide in every room at once,


*simply*

*because*

*We*

*can*

.

## LIFE IS MOSTLY QUIET

Believe me, you don't have to know.

Not so much that you render yourself helpless.

Helpless in the face of what Life brings next.

So make peace with knowing very little.

About Love.

About Others.

About how life *should* be.

Make amends with how things are.

Not knowing a thing,

walk with gentle knees,

ready to drop to them at any moment

that Life dictates.

Keep an empty hand

so that it can be brought to your heart

when a grief arrives.

Make up a bed that you can fall into

as your own comforting arms.


We come to find that Life is mostly quiet –

it asks us to live by our Knowing,

*while surrendering that very same thing.*

It vibrates easily around us,

candid and benevolent.

You see, it's only when we root ourselves

solid in some Knowing again

that Life seems to have to shout –

rises,

*lovingly,*

from Its whisper.

## A GRADUATE

*Lay me down in Love.*

Anoint my thoughts in such a way

that Heaven's supply of Lovebreath

will almost run out today.


*Bless my knees with Love.*

Ready them for all those times ahead.

In me you have found a Love Soldier

and one more loyal to This cause than any.


As many ways as there are to Love,

*let me know them then.*

Let's pretend, Beloved,

that I am *already*


A

Graduate

.

## PUPPIES

I am simply dreaming a way to love everyone within

arm's reach.

I have help:

*you* come toward me

with an aching in your eyes

and a sadness leftover in your smiles.


In this new dream I am dreaming for me

I include *all* of *you*.

Do you want to know what *my* love is?

It is *your* love.

And all of us

*Puppies*

curling into


*one*


*warm*


*heap*

# UNRELENTING GRACE

Life conspires to bless us with an

*unrelenting Grace.*

Who among us has not been touched by this generous hand,

freeing us,

one

or many layers

at a time?

*You are the lucky one*

who has known annihilation

and then absorption

back into the Love

we seek.

And it is *you* who knows

that even as the soul-cry rends your very chest

*the whole of the Universe*

*shakes*

*with Love.*

In this place of All

there is at long, long last

no place

left

to fall.

# GRIEF IS A BELL

*Grief is a bell*

*ringing throughout your heart*

*calling you to curl*
*into Yourself*
*and*
*into Another*

*until all of the notions*
*of You*
*and*
*the Ones you've lost*

*become*

*only*

*a*

*Lovesleep*

*where*

*Everyone*

dreams

thousand suns were bu

I awoke a Butterfly

wings burst into song

and I even changed my

while You were out

Planets began to dance

and all colors traded hue

turned themselves into ocea

Grasshoppers into Gazell

and I left the earth

and returned

## WHILE YOU WERE OUT

*While You were out,*
*many things transpired.*
*A sky was born.*
*Love & Laughter married.*
*Ten thousand suns were birthed.*
*I awoke a Butterfly,*
*my wings burst into song,*
*and I even changed my name*

*while You were out.*

*Planets began to dance,*
*and all colors traded hues.*
*Stars turned themselves into ocean bottoms;*
*Grasshoppers into Gazelles,*
*and I left the earth*
*and returned*

Courageous

*All*
*while You were out.*

# EVERYWHERE HEART

Heart is hiding everywhere
and when I look
without eyes
I fall
immediately
into
that warm abyss
and then
the concepts
that were my crutch
the judgments
that were my prison
the armor
that was my skin
disappears

and

the heart
hides nowhere
the seeker
ceases seeking

knowing everywhere

*Everywhere Heart.*

# WILLINGNESS

*We can become lighter & lighter.*

*We can pull from the soundless sound.*

*We can sit completely still in movement.*

*We can open every cell, as wide as it can open.*

*How, you say? And I dare say:*

*by Willingness first.*

*Then Faith in the Unbelievable.*

*By Perseverance beyond your idea of it,*

*then by layer upon layer of Patience.*

*Now, Grace moves through, unannounced.*

*Now, the Unimaginable. Miracles.*

*Then Darkness. The Womb. Gestation.*

*Birth. Then Light.*

*Then Willingness again . . .*

# NOT IN THE WAY

I opened the soft-boiled egg:

ordinary

extraordinary

yolk more yellow

than a dandelion


and it entered

the field of

white plate


as quietly as a chaperone


while I


lips parted

body poised

thoughts hovering


was struck

by this innocent display

and for one single solitary

moment


was  surprisingly


not


in the way


.

# PRIMARY COLORS

*"God?"* said I,

*"How do I walk in this world and love the walking in it?"*

And God said to me,

"I have given you your Smile.
Practiced genuinely, a smile alone
will heal you, and all the world.

I have given you Tears: they are the Soul's language.
Cleanse yourself daily with these, in Joy or in Grief,
and you will heal yourself and all the world.

I have given you your Heart. Become intimate with it.
Then, you will make love with yourself, and all the world.

And I have given you Laughter, the Universal language.
If you speak it often, it can heal you and all the world.

When these gifts are the primary colors on your palette,

You will never again need words from me –


*nay* Beloved,

You will not even need to use

*your own* anymore . . . ."

# UNREASONABLY

*"Show yourself to me,"*

said I to God again.


And this is what happened next:


I became pregnant with Light.

My eyes were sunrise and sunset, both.

Freckles announced themselves planets and stars,

and beamed upon my cheeks.

Each of my lips became a kiss to the other,

my ears heard oceans of life.

Between my eyes there was an indigo wheel,

between my toes, blond fields.

My hands remembered climbing-trees,

my hair, each Lover's fingers.


And then I whispered,

*"But why have you made me* this *way?"*

And it was told to me this:

"Because I have never had Your name before,

nor heard the way You sing it.

Nor stared into the Universe through eyes like These.

Nor laughed This way, nor felt the path that These tears take.


Because I have not known These ecstasies

nor risen to These heights, nor experienced

every nuance of the Innocence

with which you create your lows.


Nor how a Heart could grow so wide,

or break so easily

or

Love

*quite so unreasonably.*"

ll right, God, that we

as perfectly planned.

Fireflies & twilight

the blended edge of su

y the time I turn to look a

from beneath

this blushing skin.

have already sent an ana

from some new heav

Beloved within me, I do

is to Me I whisper. And to

that gathers in That

# THIS KISS

It's all right, God, that we court like this:

as perfectly planned as

*Fireflies & Twilight*

at the blended edge of summer's night.

By the time I turn to look at you

from beneath

this blushing skin,

you have already sent an angel's breath

from some *new* heaven within.

Oh, Beloved within me, I *do love* Thee.

Yet, it is *to Me* I whisper! And to The All of Life that

gathers in That name!


Oh, it is *this kiss*

I

bid

Divinity

claim.

# A LIVING PLACE

Sun breaks open in my heart
without moderation.
There is *Heaven* here.

But don't ask me to come Home just yet –
don't try to summon all of this love Home

for I have only just found
*a Living Place*.
Somewhere I can put my love.

A grassy field, where on my back I lie
musing at the broad sky, knowing *I* can light it.
Why, even the stars disappear
in the making of *this* kind of love.

Oh, there are too many ways to say the same thing.
But this is why God likes to rest at my feet –

to hear
what Love will say
*next*

.

## SOUL LANGUAGE

*Speak in a Soul Language*

*so that Everyone can hear.*

Unwind *this* Story of Humanity

with a

*presence* so *precious*

even God cannot give it definition.

Practice loving so deeply

that the word for tears

becomes

"ocean"

and

the School of Compassion

becomes the

World's Greatest Institution.

Let no one walk alone

with this journey that is

Ours

to share.

*Speak in a Soul Language,*

*so that Everyone can hear.*

## GO OUTSIDE AND PLAY

"Go outside and play,"

said God.

"I have given you Universes as fields to run free in!

And here - take this and wrap yourself in it –

It's called *LOVE*

and it will always, *always* keep you warm.

And stars! The sun and the moon and the stars!

Look upon these often, for they will remind you of

your own light!

And eyes . . . oh, gaze into every Lover's eyes;

gaze into every other's eyes

for they have given you *their* Universes

as fields to run free in.

There.

I have given you everything you need.

Now go, go, *go outside*

and

*play!*"

*forgetting*

Been turned inside
by a loss.
Drifted, like sea-wood
you're only just realize
that you are
fallible
frangible
fragile
there is a tremendous amou
that has been lost.
But
have suffered your se
been split by self-pi

# RETURNED

Our frailty *is* our humanity.

Our courage, our compass.

If you've not yet been broken open

by your *perfect* humanness.

Been turned inside out

by a loss.

Drifted, like sea-wood.

If you've only just realized

that you are

*fallible*

*frangible*

*fragile*

then there is a tremendous amount of meaning

that has been lost.

*But*

if you have suffered your *self* enough –

been split by self-pity,

by stubbornness

and pride,

*then all that was lost*

is returned to your heart

*whole, unopened, blameless, free*

## I COWER, SOMETIMES

*As is the case with Us,*

*I make*

*and You break asunder*

*whatever comfort I had constructed.*

*Never certain*

*what You want from Me,*

*believing all I am told*

*about how it is that*

*Life is supposed to be our Unfolding Joy,*

*I cower sometimes*

*God*

*in the corner, like an animal*

*who doesn't understand the thunder.*

*Who doesn't understand the lightening.*

*Who doesn't understand*

*Enlightening.*

## TO GOD

You

are my poetic device,

and I oblige You

the slightest whim.

In moonlight,

in broad daylight,

I open my legs

as Lover,

as Mother,

and I suckle the entire humanity

in Your stead.


When I was born did You say,

"This daughter, *She* is for *everyone*." –?

Then Beloved, did You place in me that lasting heart;

the sword & shield

of Love, alone?


I enter battle every day,

and love lies bleeding all around me.

I tend the wounded,

and in the tending, wound.

Sometimes truly seeing another

is lethal.

Loving fully, a bayonet.


In this Calling which you have arranged,

is the torchlight of love bright enough

that I shall see through every false idea?


Oh Beloved,


*do not leave me in darkness.*

# THREE DOGS KNOWING

They don't set out to do anything grand.

They play, the three of them:

Black and Burr-ridden,

Speckled and Bright-eyed,

Sleek and Questioning.

Every morning the play continues,

tugging one another this way and that

along throughout a day.

If He sits, scratching and gazing out across

the great divide of valleys,

She will bring Him an enduring piece of hat

or garden hose

or the last fourth of a plastic ball

and drop it at His feet.

If the One with the moon-colored eyes

lies in the ivy, with sun on Her ribs

and leaves in Her ears

the other two will attack mid-dream

with nip and tug at

neck and tail.


It is pure genius and heart.


Three dogs living out The Mystery

every moment,


while it slips like water


*through all of my grasping.*

# I AM PREPARING FOR A GRIEF

I am preparing for A Grief.

I know I shouldn't think that way,

but most of us who notice

a darkening sky

first feel it

in our Soulbody.

It's not that I want

to sit down,

set aside the Chalice,

and

find words

for such a thing.

For the day breaks glorious

across my earth.

And yet

*there . . . in the distance . . .*

*that far-off rumble . . .*

e is a new perch, and

ndings ending and beg
not yet standing

w home; I am thif
vantage points all

Old questions still runn
yet new answers
move into me

in globes of ligh

# LOOSE

There is a new perch, and a nest.

There are endings ending and beginnings
not yet standing.

A new home; I am thirty-five.
Vistas, vantage points all changed.

Old questions still rumble
yet new answers
move into me

in globes of light.

What interests me most?
Awakening.
Losing my *self* in Love.
Telling a new story, and finally
no story at all.

Then, becoming sunlight

*loose*

in the fields of my life.

# SPARK

I don't know why you haven't just

let me go, God.

Beloved, I am no match for the kind of beauty that

so many others

so easily know.


*You have made me one part Feast and one part Famine.*

Would not all of one

or all of the other

have provided

this Soul

with

whatever has been decided was lacking?


Make me a drunkard who never wakes.

Make me entirely mean, or entirely dark.

But do not set a beacon of light within me

that beckons to others

of some wholly

Holy

spark.

# HOPE'S OPPOSITE

What happened was this:
*I was brought into Hope*
*and moved within her*
*in unbridaled joy . . .*

*Then, walking naked*
*along a pleasant path,*
*I brushed by many heavens*
*until a darkness fell*
*and I was visited*
*by something that must have been*
*Hope's opposite.*

*It is between these worlds*
*that I now exist—*
*with one hand having beckoned,*
*while the other has*
*dismissed.*

# TO LOVE YOURSELF

To Love yourself, start here:

take your own hand – put it to your lips

then

lay the soft of your cheek to the round of your shoulder

where

the faint musk

of the enduring dreams and the labors of your life

perfume you.

It's a start.

It's a beginning.

Now the ache of your heart

*has*

*a*

*surface*

.

# LATELY, LIFE

Maybe I want too much from you,

but you ask too much from me, too.

There are times, if I am to be honest,

that you press your lips against mine

*and I cringe.*

Lately, Life, it has gone this way.

But We have danced millennia like this.

And there comes a time again, Life,

when I pine for you, even yearn for your touch,

wanting again, too much.

But that is when your touch, it becomes heavy again.

And when we walk, our hands no longer fit . . .

why must you and I go on like this?

*Opening and Closing the fist like this?*

*Opening and Closing*

*the fist?*

# RISE TOGETHER

It's a beautiful time to be alive.

And the long walk home is peopled –

*We* are *everywhere*.

Yet the struggle to *surrender* is where we often walk

alone.

So the next time you fall

look

to either side where you lie

and take the hand

of your dear Brother or Sister

whose own face is muddied.

We can rise together,

even if we fall alone –

for it's a beautiful time to be alive

*even*

*on this*

*long*

*walk*

*home*

.

# A KIND OF GRATITUDE

Glass-eyed, slow and thick as molasses,
but the morning shakes a gentle fist at me, anyhow.

What other creature lives this life
all the while railing against it?
The sun plays in the grass, the trees stretch . . .
every beginning of blossom and bud,
every curl of leaf, becomes even more of itself
in the hill and swale of crops
that blanket the valley.
Even the earth worms, blind and cold, seem to
burrow their simple lives with a kind of gratitude.

And me:
motionless; emotionless,
an effort to sit up straight or smile,
while all around me

Caged Birds

*singing.*

And now it is so quiet
Only the guilt of loving
wholehearted living
unabashedly,
resides.

in God's holy name
the societal stick of
over my knee
all in the name of

I cast my gaze around
like a fisherman's
It is a prayer,
it is a vociferation

# THIS LOVER

And now it is so quiet here.
Only the guilt of loving
wholeheartedly;
unabashedly,
resides.

Who in God's holy name am I –
breaking the societal stick of integrity
over my knee
all in the name of *Love*?

I cast my gaze around me
like a fisherman's net.
It is a prayer;
it is a vociferation
to my god
who wants me
*to love, and to love,*
and to at all costs
*Love*.

And now it is so quiet here,
with only

*This* lover

residing.

# WHAT IS IT THAT YOU WERE GIVEN?

What is it that you were given?

I mean from the loss.

After, what was taken.

That very thing you could never live without.

The person or place;

the secret, or circumstance -

now that it is gone,

or has been found out,

and you can no longer call *it* foundation

*what is it that you were given?*

You know, and I know, this:

there is a hollowing out.

Something comes and opens you up

right

down

the

middle

and from that moment on
*you are no longer immune to this world.*

You wake, you wander,
every familiar, now a foreign.
You walk as through water
until you make it back to your bed
and finally, even there –
your sheets; your own pillow's scent different,
as if daily someone repaints your room, displaces something,
disturbs a cherished memento.

(o

You see,
sometimes we *are* emptied.
We are emptied
because
*Life wants us to know*

*so*

*much*

*more*

*Light.*

# DIVINE SILENCES

I wait for the time, God,

when we shall greet

each other

in the reflection

of

*every soulwater into which I gaze.*

For now

I keep my faith in

Us

by honoring

every one of

Our

*Divine*

*Silences*

# NAPTIME

We need breaks.

Days where nothing disturbs the fantasy.

Where we're allowed to believe that we'll have all the

time we need

to play out desires; rehash every misery and failing.


Days where the sky is blue, the temperature perfect,

everyone complimentary

and our waistline

just where we like it.


Nights when the food is good, the wine superb;

lovers, kind and generous.

Where sleep is quiet and dreamless

and peace, a filmy veil across the planet.


We need this dream –

like naptime in kindergarten,

with someone more knowledgeable

than us saying

*it's okay,*

*go ahead,*

*be asleep.*

# THE MADRONE TREE

For some reason or another
I looked up and out from my cluttered history
just in time to see Her –


unfurling the long, copper skins of her body


like prayer flags;


like an exhalation.


And she seemed to say to me


*Have you no decency –*
*standing there, clothed in your many concepts?*


*Disrobe yourself from that constant thinking.*
*Become as naked as you began.*


*If you must,*
*clear your two clouded eyes*

*bend*

*your stiff knees*

*and throw up every laughter*

*high into the clear*

*forest*

*air!*

There.

*Now* that

*would be*

something.

# EVEN THE BODY (ILLNESS)

You have to be willing to die.

Not just surrender.

Not even just

stand in the line of fire, or

on the firing line

or stare

directly down the barrel.

You have to be willing to

Give.

Everything you think you have.

So fiercely.

So dumbly, that

*even the body*

believes it.

surrender to our hand

t has been done by our

der to the life that shows

and the lines of the map

of disappointment. The cra

everything we thought we

e things we now unders

lly we surrender to some

something deeper.

because we are worrin

but mostly

because we are tired

# ANY GOD

We surrender to our hands, finally.

To what has been done, by our own hands.

We surrender to the life that shows up on them.

*All* the grooves and the lines of the map of our body.

The creases of disappointment.  The crow's feet of joy.


We surrender to everything we thought we could manage

and to those things we now understand we can't.

And finally we surrender to something higher,

something deeper,

not because we are convinced,

but mostly


*because we are tired.*


Tired of playing at playing god.

Weary from warring with our selves.

Dusty from the many fields of Confusion

and the countless crossroads of Regret.

And so we surrender, finally.

To What Is.

And to What Was.


And to *any god*,

who will still have us.

# THIS SUN

There is quiet where the heart breaks.

Even appealing to God for love is
a step outside the hallowed ground,
and a noise that breaks the silence.

I always knew that Love would find me,
but I didn't dream that this was how:

A Brightening, happening from a place *within*,
removing every darkness.

The Universe is loyal, and patient, and
lifetimes has it watched me grow . . .

ever toward *this* sun.

# THE DAY IS COLD

Today I want to give up.

After reading Raymond Carver.

After too much wine last night.

It's not yet 9 a.m.

and the day is cold.


Closing one's eyes offers an abyss

and a place to fall into.


But isn't that what this is?


Everyone stumbling

- drinking, spilling -


everyone wanting to be saved


*just a little.*

## LET ME APOLOGIZE

We truly are

One Nation, Of God,

Indivisible

*because we cannot divide the One Heart*

no matter what we may say or do

to one another.

But let *me* apologize

to every god for what we've done

in That name.

Let *me* apologize

to every People, for what we've each believed

as we took a life.

Let *me* apologize

for every One who has forgotten Oneness.

For conquests. For slavery. For war.

For conversions and missions.

For the harming of animals, and the rape of

peoples and Planets.

Let *me* apologize

for The Guilty

who don't even know

*Their Innocence.*

perform Itself Here

t the Histories change,

unrequited love. shall b

ery broken wing made

f History begins Itself N

and You are maker o

are neither brick nor

t a Dreamer of what's

ld may not even need

ecoration. On oceans

t's not even decide on

# THIS HISTORY

Let the Histories change, then.

If a Red Sea was ever truly parted

then let the same kind of miracle

perform itself Here.

Let the Histories change, then.

Every unrequited Love shall be requited.

Every broken wing made whole.

A History begins Itself Now

and You are maker of It.

You are neither brick nor bauble

but a Dreamer of what's Next.

*This* World may not even need Foundation. Or Decoration.

Or Oceans to manage.

*Let's not even decide on a name*

but let the Histories change Now,

all the same.

## BEAUTIFUL LIFE, BASTARD LIFE

Today, you beautiful life, you bastard life,
you tore out nearly all of my seams.

But your ardent pursuit of revealing to me
my True Nature

is applauded.

When I can stand again, I will congratulate you properly.

Just now, I am still getting used to all of the
new places where life can reach into me.

All of the spaces
where Grief and Dreams
have tumbled out,

just so much fluff and batting having revealed

yet

another

Child

of

God

.

## PRECIOUS WATERS RUN

Emerging from the ground of Being,

it's as if we haven't yet got wings or

armoring to protect us

from encounters that will mostly feel

*like suffering.*

As innocent as water, We Happen.

We pool or we run, singing and whispering

over the jagged and timeworn stones to

Awakening.

But it's as if the mother who birthed us

*never named us.*

Trusted us too much.

Expected us to parent ourselves

and then, all the world.

And so These Precious Waters, They run:

*pooling and running*
*singing and whispering*
*crying and keening*

*to the Sea.*

*Crying and keening*
*to the Sea . . .*

# THE GREAT SILENCE

I am being opened by
the Great Silence –
every pattern uncurled
from the gripping.

In this chosen palsy,
some part of me must still believe
in consequence.

And how tenaciously I have clung.
Even to the point of imagining
that *I am That*
to which I cling.

Yet this is no great discovery.
Lifetimes are spent so compromised:
moments run through by thought,
and Silence, only an occasional comma
throughout a long sentence . . .

# NOT YOUR SONG

That is enough for now.

Fall silent,

for *this*, *is not* Your song.

Turn your eyes inward and let your mouth remain closed;

your tongue soft and quiet

until you are sure –

quite sure

that you are done.

Then,

*re-string* Your instrument, dear One.

before, I touch the Hea

I will stride into any

te it to enter me, with
simple darkness.


I traffic and I trave
rough the last of the s


to This Day

am entering my own hea
that All light longs ag
for any darkness

# ALL LIGHT LONGS

I hope that there comes a time

when I will not have to touch the Wound

before I touch the Heart.


When I will stride into any abyss

and invite it to enter me, with Its

simple darkness.


I traffic and I travel

through the last of the shadows


to This Day

when I am entering my own Heart so completely

that all Light longs again

for *any* darkness.


For any simple darkness at all.

# THREADBARE PLACES

There is so much I want to tell you
A story you will never hear

The journey Home is so precarious
that only those of us who are stepping
remember our moments of grace
and the paper-thin width
of the line that is walked
between This world and That one

If I were to unwind it before you
To speak of the bends in the road
Those places where no path is visible
Where no light glows
If I were to unravel the tapestry
Show you the threadbare places
Where there was soullessness
Where there was void

If you were to stop asking

If you were to start holding

If you were to begin seeing

If you were able to accept

If you were ready


I could let my head rest in your lap

Saying nothing at all

of what is surely ahead

for you

to meet


There are enough teachers before me

who tell my story

There is enough family abroad

who ask nothing and offer everything

It is Their map that I follow


*It is the godless*
*finding God*

# WEIGHTLESS

We are like the turtle

who moves along the cracked earth

unable to look up

although it knows the sun exists.

We carry the lifetimes' burden

of our personality

like an apology.

We search for a way

to somehow see the stars

or turn ourselves into the

Pheonix

of

Truth

yet for all of our prayers

there is only the ground

and our barren earth of self-recriminations.

But

finally

*something, someone*

steps into our path

finally

*something, someone*

speaks

the one word we need


to lift us up

to carry us


*destined and deserving*


to the water's edge

to our Oceanhome

where the lover's scent was left

where the arms of the waves caress

where we glide


*weightless*


beneath the shell.

# WITH YOUR WILL

What would You tell me?

That I am good?

That my worthiness is not even up to me?

That there is a shaft of light

too bright to look at,

too hot to hold?

That it exists in me

and it is *You*?

That it cannot make everything 'better'

but that it can make it seem

more precious?

That my life is a buffet set for Heaven & Earth

and Angels prepare a concert

in my name?

What else, *God*,

would you tell me?

That I am Love?

That this is not a job?

Not a sentence,

and do not make it so?

That my life will move with Truth and with Light

and that no one need understand this but

*Me* and *You?*

*But how, God?*

*How* do I lift a foot from this moment

into the next?


(๏


*"With your will I lift it for you.*

*With*

*your*

*will*

*I lift your entire life for you."*

*naked*

everyone will know

that

each

passing

moment

...tains the changing s...

...dout we cling to as se...
...must let go of to grow...

...just champion to take
...fall in love with as te...

# WE ARE AWAKENING ONE ANOTHER

We are awakening one another.

It does not matter whose heart

still clings to the vine.

In time

*everyone will know*

that

each

passing

moment

contains the changing seasons.

That what we cling to as seed

we must let go of to grow.

Must champion to take root.

Must fall in love with as tender shoot.


*Spring, summer, winter, fall*


this is *All* . . .


yet hearts do cling.



They do.

# US

I want to write about Love.

I want record

of how it feels to be in the embrace of a trembling.

To drink from hands that shake.

I want to lay into the Infinite that moment

when the heart finds it feels nothing

but quakes

at what it may.

I want to remember every footstep & stumble;

every vista & valley,

and every time I shall release my gripping,

so that Love

does not suffocate.

I want to write


about


Us.

## THIS IS A DIAMOND

It is clear that This
is a Diamond.
Multifaceted.  Faces of God.


Each time I see you now
I have only two choices:
break open
or
openly break.


How can I explain *This*?
It might be easier
if we
leave the castle
climb the walls
enter the city
and let Our Love be made
in

*all* of God's streets.

## THERE IS A WORD FOR THIS

There is a word for this
and I don't
yet
know it.

You say my name
and a star
tumbles from the sky.

You rest your eyes in mine
and the sun, rising,
pauses.

You lie beside me
in this womb
of silence, and
Time
offers itself to us
like melon.

*There is a word for this*

And

I

don't

yet

know

it

.

## A LOVE LIKE THIS

Inspire a Loyalty within me.


When I come to you, open.

When I run to you, stand.

Engender in me that thing

that moves mountains

parts seas

raises the Pheonix

brings a village to the water's edge.


Cause me to become manifest

in ways that no one has yet seen . . .


*a love like this* could do that.

# GOD REDEEMS

You are that kind of creature that isn't tamed:

a storm moves through, a sky opens

and

drenched, running for shelter, *I am laughing*.

I wait to see what morsel falls next

sated simply by one taste of you.

Do you know how I know that
I am alive?

*Because you see me.*

*And I want to be seen.*

☙

God redeems, oh how

God redeems.

# ANCIENT ONE

You moan my name
You speak my name
You make my name

An Ancient Tongue

You come inside
You move inside
You live inside

This Ancient Song

You draw me in
You breathe me in
You hold me in

An Ancient Womb

*You speak me*
*Moan me*
*Make me*
*Move me*
*Live me*
*Love me*

Ancient One

you awaken, dream
an afterglow of Glo
one more poem.
...re I leave pen & p
at bed's edge.
...re I pass my ring
from my finger to f
inside your own.
Before I take the
...ol white sheet
from your shoulder
and exchange it for

# ONE MORE POEM

*One more poem.*

Before I come back to bed.

Before I return to you, naked.

Before you awaken, dreamfilled

in an afterglow of God

*one more poem.*

Before I leave pen & paper

at bed's edge.

Before I pass my ring

from my finger to place it

inside your own.

Before I take the

cool white sheet

from your shoulders

and exchange it for the

wet warm invitation

of my Heaven

*One*

*more*

*poem.*

## WE ARE UNREQUITED, MY LOVE

We are Unrequited, my Love.

I wish that your hands

had never touched my hair.

That I had only seen your name,

never held the face.

I wish that each of your glances

had not opened a hunger in me.

That the time I let my fingers pass

down the cool sides of your neck,

across the warm house of your heart,

that you would have shunned me;

that I would have run.


I wish that our hands

had never entwined –

that I would never have created


languages & symbols


in your moistening palm –

that someone would have seen us,

that someone would have come.


I wish that you had never

uttered my name aloud, or

written it down, or whispered it

alone in the night.

That I would never have

held your gaze

across the room, so many times –

that I would have hesitated to come,

that I would have hurried to go.


I wish that my lust for you

would turn to ashes –

that my want for the knowledge of you,

for the sound of you crying out,

would disappear like smoke,


and that the thought of you inside me

– or anywhere in the world –

did not frighten,

and that the risk

of toppling the lives we live did not


strobe like a beacon amidst these churning,

relentless seas . . .


*but we are Unrequited*, my Love.

## TOO THIRSTY NOW

I will write you a poem:

The Earth waits for our Eyes.
A Hawk, for the Dawn.
A Child, for the Lap.
The Heart, for Presence.

Mystery, waits for our Parting.
Lust, for our Reunion.
Hunger, for one Taste of you.
Grief, a Reason to break.

I wait for *anything*
that reminds me
of
You,

too thirsty now,
*even to drink.*

# GOODBYE

I know you have decided to withdraw,

and that is sound, so sound.

At least one of us understands the consequence.

I am too lost even to cry for help.

God delivered You

so close . . . so close

and now I slip into a world

between worlds,

far worse than Hell.

I call it "Mundane".


You see, You . . . *You* became Heaven.


There is no fault here.

One of us *should* rise up,

face every demon,

stretch the wing

*and*

*fly*

*away.*

## WE JUST WANT LOVE

Everything
you thought you wanted –

so did I.

As it turns out,
funny,
*we just want love.*

Aspirations and lofty notions call –
funny,
*we just need love.*

Knowing you very little
I feel as if I know you well:

the moan beneath the chest,
the pleading in the eyes . . .
one giant asking
of a yet unformed question.

One answer surely,
in many forms will come.
And I will say its name.
And I will call it:

Love.

word is a finger of God, te
...ning every unveiling to
..., I cannot say much —
...are here is new life bef
...olar systems, planets t
...it can be called, " Th
...willing party: your

...orning I came out onto
...own that Tangled
...e to the water's edge a
Saltwater streamed
and the Heart

## THAT FINE CHAPERONE

My Love, only You can bring me Home now.
You and that fine chaperone, Annihilation.

Each delicate word is a finger of God, teasing me open,
furthering every unveiling to You.

Beloved, I cannot say much – I dare not.
What we have here is new life before Us.
Galaxies, solar systems, planets to sustain –
all of it can be called, "The Heart".
I am a willing party: your loyal pilgrim.

☉

This morning I came out onto the shoreline
from that Tangled Jungle.
I came to the water's edge and I knelt down.
Saltwater streamed from my eyes,
and the Heart, It said,

*"I am Your Child.*
*I am your Innocent, Naked Child,"*

It said.

# CLOTHING & SOAP

We show up as

clothing & soap

groomed, plucked, shaven

hopeful.


We wonder if love is real

or if it will dissolve

like sugar

touching water.


Meanwhile,

beneath this costumery


Sings a Man.

Writes a Woman.

# IN A NEW YORK APARTMENT

In a New York apartment

on an Easter Sunday

with pigeons cooing

and thin clouds passing

over Brownstone buildings

and my New York Times

and taxis shouting


with still-tired feet

from yesterday's walking

and two new perfumes

– one on each wrist –

with sidewalks still vacant

and stoops still shaded


my lover sleeps


in a New York apartment


on last night's bedclothes

damp from our couplings

stained with our loving

rich with our scent


with everything opened

and nothing contained



in a New York apartment


where my lover sleeps

## FOR THE FIRST TIME

Hello again and for the first time, my Love.

We have braved your heart, and mine.

We have traversed terrain

rougher than our ancestors,

more formidable

than setting out

toward a far off horizon

and the imaginings

that breed all dread.


We have discovered

with our own eyes

and our own hearts

that the worlds we create

within & without

are not flat;

that, indeed, when we reach their horizons

we not only extend beyond them,

rounding their soft, watery spheres,

but that they pull us gently

onward toward the limitless

sunsets and sunrisings

where we shall meet

again and again

for the first time, my Love.

# IF WE ARE NAKED

*We say that we will have a Good Life.*

This is a guarantee

if we are kind to one another.

If we are patient.

If, when I speak, you listen,

and if when you speak, I hear you.

This is assured,

if we continue to look for one another.

If we want to find.

If, when I am here, I am seen,

and if, when you are here, I see you.

*We say that this will be a Good Life.*

This is a guarantee

if we are Naked with one another.

If we are clotheless.

If, when I am vulnerable,

you shelter,

and if, when you are defenseless,

*I protect.*

# ALL OF YOU

I want to know you like That.

Like a poet describes a foreign land –

*Neruda: an open mouth on her breast*

*the moonlight  the surface of the water*

*the pillars of light  the musk of her earth . . .*


More than the deep of your eyes

I want to know what they see

when you are moved to kiss me,

when you must have me;

when jealousy burns you to ashes.

I want to know you

like a mother knows her child suffers

ten thousand miles away.

I want to know the

ache and sour of your fear

of losing us

and what the fight tastes like

on your tongue.

I want to know what demons say to you

in your long nights

and what happened on that day

and how you've forgotten

and how you've forgiven.


I want to know you like This:


that as you sit casually

taking me in,

smiling playfully,

there is always

*all of you*

begging

me


for my heart.

open all of the windows
so that God can come and

I know why God takes su
in this House I call

This place
where hearts come
to be broken

end of the Long Day I
God? Why, hearts to be bro

And God always rep

Never broken, dear Lo

# NEVER BROKEN

I am my own Home, now.

Wherever I move

the Light –

It moves with me.

I open all of the windows and the doors

so that God can come and go, easily.

I don't know why God takes such delight

in this House I call "Me".

This place

where hearts come

to be broken.

At the end of the Long Day I always ask,

"God? *Why*, hearts to be broken?"

And God always replies,

"Never broken, *dear Lover* –

only *Opened*."

# HIGHER

Each question that you asked me –

I pretended to know the answer.

I was truthful

but I was

*blinded*

by the expanding sky

behind you

and its colors on your skin

*distracted*

by the shift

of one knee over the other

your hands draped

like contented lovers

and how you gave every light in the room

your eyes.

I was present

but I was


*taken*


by the honey in your voice

by the nectar in your words


*preoccupied*


with petty desires

that pulsed in me

daring me

to cross the room

and open your dream

and take you


*Higher*

# I HAVE MADE YOU CRAZY

*I have made you crazy*, I know.

But My Love, you have come Home now.

*Everything*, just as you left it:

my breasts, full and warm,

my nipples, cool and firm.

You have traveled far –

climbed and descended many mountains.

And the lantern in the window, I have placed it there

*for You.*

Now, your hand on the doorknob,

now a softness under the feet.

My smooth thighs, my round flesh,

my musk and my wet

awaiting you, and all of you entering me.


*I have made you crazy*, I know.


But God has made us Crazy, too.

# IS IT ENOUGH?

*Is it enough, my Love*

*that I love you?*
*Here, between each line,*
*all that is beyond*
*what we right now know of love,*
*exists.*

*I might look into Your eyes*
*to try to find it.*
*I might rest within them*
*and*
*wait.*

*But is it enough, my Love*
*that I love you?*
*And that what we don't yet know of love*

*exists?*

# LEAVING HOME

*We had forgotten how to love.*
*It was only days; moments,*
*but they maimed Us.*

You wandered through Our city
from face to face,
searching for Me there.
You came and You went
leaving Our home –
haggard, hungry

a beggar for Love-Alms.

I wandered through some city
from street to street,
looking for You there.
I came and I went
leaving The Home
hollowed, fatigued
desperate for peace –

a monk, outside her temple.

*We remembered how to love.*
*It was only days; moments,*
*but they saved Us.*

## WHAT LOVE ISN'T

Hark!
A thirty-two year old
is coming into her Becoming.
If he strips the limb of all its leaves
a fruit will ripen –
prettier now than it might have been.

I never knew
how one half-gesture could contain
the power of a storm
or how a passion could disembowel me
like a soft creature taken suddenly from the deep,
splayed, open bellied,
eyes unblinking

In All This Love.

There is a kind of glory, you know –
in staying.
Like the pride of keeping one's own teeth
though they may ache and yellow,

and how all the world *loves* a hero!

But no one ever tells you
that *this*
is how we die . . .

# LIGHTBEAMS

There was that moment when our souls paused.

There was a second of contemplation;
a weighing of all the odds, but
conversations filled our ears again
and everyone had continued eating,
so we lifted the food to our mouths
as if nothing had passed,
as if what I asked
and how you answered
hadn't broken our hearts at all.

And I took one more bite,
even after I had witnessed
such a longing in you, that it simply
could not let us look away.
I wondered then, if you would
remember me, and if I would
ever forget, this living, wordless
moment between two paired souls.

I wanted to take you, hold you, and

give you *the one thing you had never had*,

but that empty place in you –

it also dwells in me.

Neither one of us can offer anything

but condolences.


So then, we will be Mirrors.

I will reflect to you your Wholeness,

all of your Light, and the many ways you love.

And You, You will dance *lightbeams*

across my breast . . .

rivulet, or a river

Sprinkling or spate

it doesn't matter

...atever it is you want

whatever it is I se...

that You need

willingness to surren...

is so new a creatur...

...t I wouldn't even kno...

And should It lea...

...om the forest of my...

...nd gut me...

I wouldn't

## SO NEW A CREATURE

*A rivulet, or a river;*

*sprinkling, or spate –*

*it doesn't matter.*

*Whatever it is You want next.*

*Whatever it is I see*

*that You need.*

*The willingness to surrender*

*is so new a creature, that*

*I wouldn't even know Its colors.*

*And should It leap,*

*from the forest of my pride*

*and gut me –*

I wouldn't

feel

a

thing.

# LIKE WE ARE

Before I even conjure it

You answer.

I try to say 'I Love You'

and my own face

– wonder of wonders –

appears before

my Heart.


So I wait for the dawn.

Thinking that if I lie

still as a baby bird

curled in the egg

You

will come,

ushered by The Calling,

out from the face of the deep,

where Darkness & Dawning

are still deciding,


*like We are,*


where One begins and the Other ends.

# OUR ANSWERING

You sleep, having slipped softly

from within me

only moments ago.

You will rest, and I will write.

The half-light of this moment

creates an oil painting

of the tousled bed sheets

and your form.

It is a Naked Day.

And your eyes

were just upon me.

And the words of our dawn have

been making love

for hours.

When you wake, we will drive somewhere.

We will keep the wolves of our lives at bay, and stay

at the water's edge . . .

I know that God is Calling.

I know, I know, I *know* this.

But tell God

that *this*, *too*, is a part of Our Answering.

# EVERY FOOTSTEP

Is it *you* who speaks first?

When the veils lay or lift

is it *me* who initiates it?

When a longing returns Beloved,

is it *you* who first feels it?

My Other, I cannot even laugh

without wondering if *you* laugh, too.

I cannot cry

without then reaching out to touch *your* cheek.

And when I leave the heart

and enter forgetting

I try not to look for you there . . .


but you are the beginning

and I am the ending

of every footstep.

*Every footstep.*

# IS IT THEN?

*When will I see You again?*
*Is it when a Christ returns?*
*Is it when the Light*
*is eclipsed?*
*Is it when the Seasons falter?*
*Is it when the Beast falls,*
*or when the Creatures scatter?*
*Is it when the Earth breaks*
*and the Ice runs?*
*Is it when the Oceans thirst*
*and when Mountains roar?*
*Is it when the Silence wails*
*or the Prayer dies?*
*Is it when*
*the Nectars run*
*from the Opening of the Womb*
*to cover*
*your*
*Naked Heart?*


*Is it Then?*

Oneself,

except

perhaps

through the passagewa

of

the Heart?

Me, In Here, Out There

Love ocean

would ask you to kiss my

but you might even

The One

crying them

## LOVEOCEAN

You are beyond sex to me.

You see, I used to want only for you

to enter me

fully.

But how does one enter

Oneself,

except

perhaps

through the passageway

of

the Heart?


You, Me, In Here, Out There:

it has all become the same


LoveOcean.


I would ask you to

kiss my fresh tears


but You

might even be

The One crying them . . .

# THIS KIND OF LOVE

This kind of love –

it is an *organic*

thing.


Its footfall is quiet,

like a camel's in the desert.

Or the thick, white, silence of snow.


*And It waits* –

in the deep of the eyes,

until that moment It is finally seen.


And this kind of love –


it means standing tall in the bare wind.

Even as the clouds disband.

Even as the warm sun finally claims you –


*yes,*


even then.

# THAT GOD MAY PASS

Last night we made this pact:

that we would sew the seeds of light

into the earth of us

coaxing

each life to move

from within to without,

deepening

such an opening

that God may pass


between these hearts


that God

may

pass

.

## IS LOVE

The only thing that comes between us

are varying shades of light, Beloved.

Our bodies have become more like planets

heavy in their orbit

and keeping us from meeting as closely as we desire.

We have coupled again

while the sun sits high in the February sky

and while everyone else remains busy - loyal to the lists

in their hands.

But our own rest open

upon bedsheets and pillows,

and our bodies are entwined in as many symbols as there

are for


*Divine*


◎


Hurrying toward nothing

the only thing worth answering is Love.

Happening into Loving

the only thing worth being

is Love

is Love

is Love.

## FOR STILL, I LOVE

*Yesterday*

*You drew a breath of*

*Hallelujah*

*from this woman's tired body*

*so withdrawn*

*into her own heart*

*that the body*

*had ceased*

*to beat.*

*With weary*

*and compassionate hands*

*with the salt*

*of your Sisyphean journey*

*you loved*

*and I was tended*

*by the only attendant*

*of this heart.*

*Yesterday*

*I drew the seed*

*of Hallelujah*

*from deep within*

*that viscera of your grief*


*and it came forth*

*pungent*

*full of your life*

*keening*

*for all that had passed*

*yet saying*


*no*

*I cannot be lost*


*for still*


I love

# EARTHBOUND

There are
universes and stars hidden within me
and
He finds them.

I try to understand what this blessing means:

why the same god who lets me suffer
has also let me soar.

You see
I didn't know how many dreams I carried
until
One by One

He has delivered them into Him

innocent & dreamy as any Dream is
that leaves its Heaven
to willingly
fall
to
the
Earth

He has become dizzy and drunken from my nectar
having romanced it from its keep,
and I am released
into far-off galaxies
and spun so softly open,
while He waits
for
my
return.

©

I wonder if He knows
that this is when I make a deal again,
with God again:

to twirl into this heavy land
and stay upon the touching of it.

Fall into this heavy land
and somehow

*love*

the touching of it.

An arc was begun,
a covenant made,
a promise fulfilled

...night we ushered ...
The New Beginning
of a New World
by making new love
in as many ways
as we could find

And today ~
...ay I want desperately ...
how else to say,

I love you,

# HONEYMOON

The world wants us to find a New Way, my Love –

for *Loving*.

So We answer.

I saw you, and knew God.

You saw me, and knew Everything.

Lightening, thunder, great rains ensued.

An arc was begun,

a covenant made,

a promise fulfilled.


Last night we ushered in

The New Beginning

of a New World

by making *new* love

in as many ways

as we could find.

And today –

today I want desperately to know

how else to say,


"I Love You."

# IF YOU GO FIRST

If You go first

and I am alone and have only our music

and the wine I open with my own hand

I will lay in our bed

in the middle

and wait for Your serenade, my Love.


Before I retire and begin to conjure

the sweet inhale of our intimacy

I will run my fingertips down the milk of my breast

trail them along the curve of my thigh

dusting the dream of Us in all of those places

where only the two of us traveled.

I will make real again how we became

so close that I could rest against you anywhere

saying to you even,

"Beloved - there will be nectars upon you,

come morning."

# ALL FOR LOVE

All for the Dream & the Glory.

All for the right to choose.

All for something to live for.

All for something to lose.

All for the Bite in the Beauty.

All for the Beast in the Bone.

All for the Spirit and Flesh

being married

with

*Love*

as

the Sword

in

the Stone.

## THAT'S ALL

The liberation; the freedom that comes.

Oh, Beloved how I live now!

Even with the storm, obvious and impending,

*You are what I want.*

Who cares for society, or logic,

or the heart's history of throwing

every practicality

to life's winds.

*It is simply what happens;*

what strikes the soul.

And down on our knees we feel

the sword on the shoulder.

Oh, never let a person tell you how life will be.

They haven't *lived.* They haven't *risked.*

*They haven't met the One Who Meets Them.*


That's all.

Raised in the Pacific Northwest, American poet *Em Claire* now makes her home in Ashland, Oregon with her husband and family. Her works are her autobiography . . . and in some ways may be the autobiography of all of us.